From bear to brawn

sexy

/ˈsɛksi/

Learn to pronounce

adjective

1. 1.

sexually attractive or exciting.

"sexy French underwear"

synonyms:

sexually attractive, seductive, desirable, alluring, inviting, sensual, sultry, slinky, provocative, tempting, tantalizing; nubile, voluptuous, shapely, luscious, lush;

feline;

bedroom;

flirtatious, coquettish;

*informal*hot, fanciable, beddable, come-hither, come-to-bed;

*informal*fit, peng;

*informal*foxy, cute, bootylicious;

*informal*spunky;

*vulgar slang*fuck-me

"she's so sexy"

erotic, arousing, exciting, stimulating, hot;

sexually explicit, titillating, suggestive, racy, risqué, provocative, spicy, juicy, adult, X-rated;

rude, coarse, smutty, pornographic, vulgar, crude, lewd, lubricious;

*informal*raunchy, steamy, naughty, horny, porno, blue, skin;

*informal*saucy, fruity;

*informal*gamy

"a TV show featuring sexy home videos"

AKUMA

GYM
SPORTSBAR

GILBERT

©2018

©2018

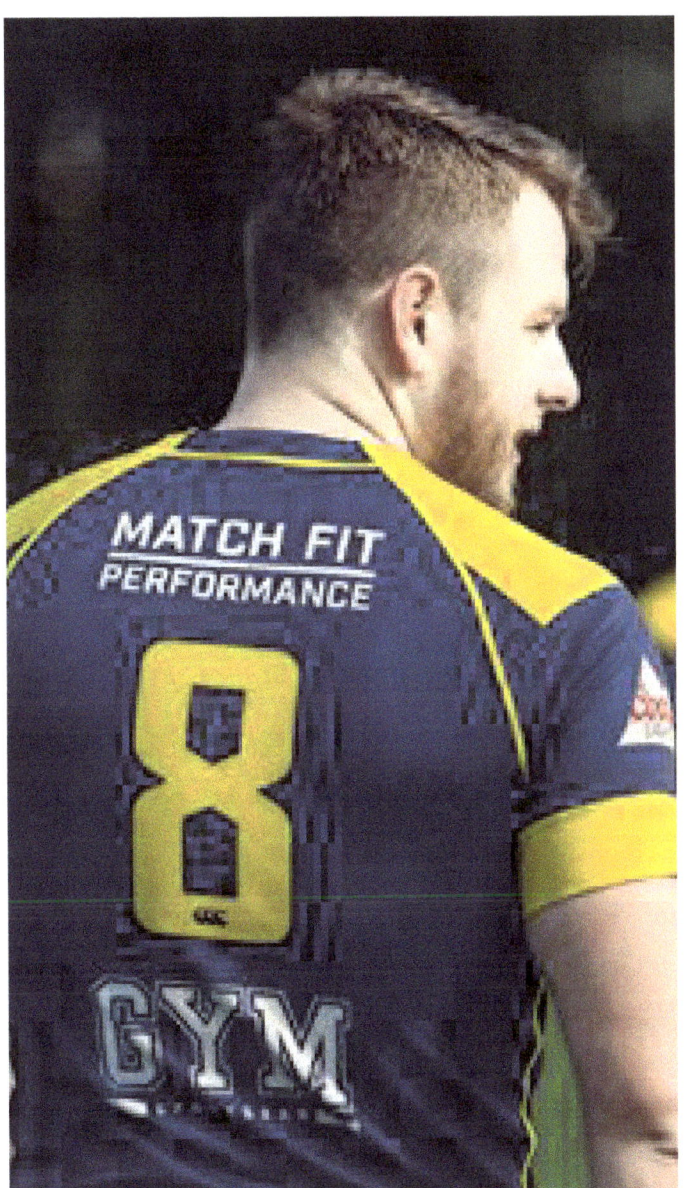